HEAVEN

By
George Beiderwieden

Concordia Publishing House
St. Louis, Mo.

"IS there a heaven?" "Can the teaching of the Bible regarding heaven be true?" "Where is heaven?" These are questions which confront us as death takes from us loved ones who are very near and dear to us. It is quite natural that the aching heart should be filled with grief. Even Jesus, our Lord, shed tears of sorrow at the grave of His friend Lazarus. But we Christians have a comfort which truly comforts. For us there is "a balm of Gilead" which can and does heal the wounds of our sorrowing hearts. Thank God, we Christians know that our dear ones have gone to heaven, where "the wicked cease from troubling and the weary be at rest." (Job 3:17)

For the believing Christian, who accepts without question what the Bible has to say, to think of heaven is sweet and most comforting contemplation. He delights in it. He loves to hear about it. He frequently talks about it with such as are equally interested in it. Heaven is the goal he hopes to atttain. Heaven is the home he expects to occupy in all eternity. "If I only get to heaven!" is the sincere and fervent wish of his heart.

It must be borne in mind that whatever knowledge we have of heaven is obtained solely from the Bible, God's own revelation of spiritual and heavenly things to man. The Scriptures are our only source of information. Without this divine revelation we would not so much as know that there is a heaven. From reason and from the moral longings and aspirations of his being man might infer and therefore hope that "death does not end all" and that, "if a man die, he shall live again." But inferences never give him certainty. If God had not spoken to us in His Word, no man could say with firm assurance, "When I die, I shall still live; for in passing out of this life I merely pass into another and eternal life." But God *has* spoken, and therefore heaven is a precious certainty to us.

Turning to God's special revelation concerning heaven, we ask:

WHAT IS HEAVEN?

According to the Bible heaven is a real, objective place. We are not to think of heaven as a mere state or condition. Speaking of heaven, Jesus says: "I go to prepare a *place* for you" (John 14:2). In the same passage He refers to it as "My Father's *house*." The Apostle John speaks of heaven as "the holy *city*." (Rev. 21:2)

WHERE IS HEAVEN?

This is a question which we are unable to answer because God has not revealed its exact location or geographical boundaries to us. According to the language of the Bible we may, however, think of it as being above us. In Ps. 103:11 heaven is spoken of as "high above the earth." Israel's appeal, according to Deut. 26:15, reads: "Look *down* from Thy holy habitation, from heaven, and bless Thy people Israel." In Deut. 3:12 the expression is used. "Who shall go *up* for us to heaven?" The psalmist exclaims: "If I ascend *up* into heaven, Thou art there" (Ps. 139:8). When Jesus left this earth, after having completed His redemptive work, the Bible tells us "He was *taken up*, and a cloud received Him out of their sight" (Acts 1:9). As the disciples stood there in amazement, gazing steadfastly up into heaven after Him, two heavenly messengers said unto them: "Ye men of Galilee, why stand ye gazing *up* into heaven? This same Jesus which is *taken up* from you into heaven shall so come in like manner as ye have seen Him go into heaven" (Acts 1:11). After this experience the disciples no doubt always thought of heaven as being above, on high. They had seen their beloved Master go up, ascending higher and higher till a cloud removed Him from their sight. Heaven to them was up above, somewhere beyond the azure blue. We, too, like to think of it in the same way.

WHAT KIND OF PLACE IS HEAVEN?

Oh, that human tongue or pen could adequately describe it! Heaven is a place of entrancing beauty, of matchless splendor, of ineffable glory. *Heaven is the habitation of God,* the capital of the divine King of the universe, the place where Jesus has gone to prepare a mansion for us. How could it be otherwise than *beautiful?*

The Apostle John, who was carried away in the spirit and permitted to view "that great city, the holy Jerusalem," gives us an authentic and, at the same time, a most thrilling description of heaven in Rev. 21. He writes: "Her light was like unto a stone most precious, even like a jasper stone, clear as crystal; and had a wall, great and high, and had twelve gates and at the gates twelve angels and names written thereon, which are the names of the twelve tribes of the children of Israel: on the east three gates, on the north three gates, on the south three gates, and on the west three gates. And the wall of the city had twelve foundations and in them the names of the twelve apostles of the Lamb. And he that talked with me had a golden reed to measure the city and the gates thereof and the wall thereof. And the city lieth foursquare, and the length is as large as the breadth; and he measured the city with the reed, twelve thousand furlongs. The length and the breadth and the height of it are equal. And he measured the wall thereof, an hundred and forty and four cubits according to the measure of a man, that is, of the angel. And the building of the wall of it was of jasper. And the city was pure gold, like unto clear glass. And the foundations of the wall of the city were garnished with all manner of precious stones. The first foundation was jasper, the second sapphire, the third a chalcedony, the fourth an emerald, the fifth sardonyx, the sixth sardius, the seventh chrysolite, the eighth beryl, the ninth a topaz, the tenth a chrysoprasus, the eleventh a jacinth, the twelfth an amethyst. And the twelve gates were twelve pearls; every several gate was of one pearl. And the street of the city was pure gold, as it were transparent glass. And I saw no temple therein; for the Lord God Almighty and the Lamb are the temple of it. And the city had no need of the sun, neither of the moon, to shine in it; for the glory of God did lighten it, and the Lamb is the light thereof. And the nations of them which are saved shall walk in the light of it; and the kings of the earth do bring their glory and honor into it. And the gates of it shall not be shut at all by day; for there shall be no night there. And they shall bring the glory and honor of the nations into it. And there shall in no wise enter into it anything that defileth, neither whatsoever worketh abomination or maketh a lie; but they which are written in the Lamb's Book of Life." (Rev. 21:11-27)

No human author has ever succeeded in describing the splendor, the grandeur, the magnificence, of heaven more eloquently and graphically than the inspired Apostle John in the passage just quoted. Heaven, according to the Bible, is a place of exquisite beauty.

WHO IS IN HEAVEN?

God is in heaven. Heaven is the dwelling place of God. King Solomon prayed on the occasion of the dedication of the Temple: "Hear Thou from Thy dwelling place, *even from heaven*" (2 Chron. 6:21). God Himself declares: *"The heaven is My throne"* (Is. 66:1). In Ps. 123:1 we read: "Unto Thee lift I up mine eyes, O Thou that *dwellest in the heavens.*" In Ps. 33:13, 14 we are told: "The Lord looketh from heaven; He beholdeth all the sons of men. *From the place of His habitation* He looketh upon all the inhabitants of the earth." What a place heaven must be since it is the home of God, the habitation of the "King of kings, the dwelling place of the Lord of lords"! His very presence makes it a place of unspeakable glory. What a rapturous and thrillingly entrancing view must have been opened up to Stephen, the martyr, who, shortly before being stoned, was given a glimpse of heaven! "But he, being full of the Holy Ghost, looked up steadfastly into heaven and saw the glory of God." (Acts 7:55)

Jesus is in heaven. When Stephen looked up into heaven, he saw "Jesus standing on the right hand of God" (Acts 7:55). The presence of Jesus makes heaven what it really is, a place of bliss and supreme joy. "The Lamb is the light thereof" (Rev. 21:23). He who loved us with an everlasting love, who sacrificed Himself and gave His life a ransom for us, is in heaven, waiting for us, longing for us; and when we get there, He will welcome us. Without Jesus heaven would lose its charm and beauty.

The story is told of a little sick child whose mother was

7

seriously ill. In order that the mother might have absolute quiet, the child was taken away to a friend's house, where a kind lady cared for her. The mother's condition, however, grew worse, and at length she died. The father said: "We'll not tell the child about Mother's departure; she is too young to remember her mother. Let her stay where she is till the funeral is over." This was done, and after a few days the little girl was brought back to the house. No mention was made of her mother or of what had occurred. But no sooner was she taken into the house than she ran first into one room, then into another. "Where is Mother?" she cried; "I want Mother!" And when they were compelled to tell her what had happened, she cried out: "Take me away, take me away! I don't want to be here without Mother." It was Mother who made it home to her.

And so it is in heaven. The fact that Jesus is in heaven makes it a place beyond compare. What an experience it will be for us to see Him "face to face"! There we shall be permitted to walk with Him and talk with Him and forever thank Him for His love. There we shall behold the nailprints in His hands, His open side — mute evidences of His sacrifical love toward us. What prospect of ectasy and happiness! In heaven we shall see Jesus.

All the holy angels are in heaven. In his vision of heaven Isaiah sees seraphim, angels of high rank and order (Is. 6:2). The prophet Daniel, in a similar vision, beholds a great multitude of angels: "Thousand thousands ministered unto Him, and ten thousand times ten thousand stood before Him" (7:10). The Apostle John reports: "And I beheld, and I heard the voice of many angels round about the throne and the beasts and the elders; and the number of them was ten thousand times ten thousand and thousands of thousands" (Rev. 5:11). What a place of ceaseless activity heaven must be with its myriads of ministering spirits, serving God and worshiping Him, doing His pleasure with holy delight, and executing His commandments for the promotion of His purposes!

The saints of God of past ages are in heaven. Think of it! We shall meet Abraham, Isaac, Jacob, Job, David, and all the rest of God's saints of former ages. In Matt. 8:11 the Lord Jesus informs us: "Many shall come from the East and West and shall sit down with Abraham and Isaac and Jacob in the kingdom of heaven." All the New Testament saints, the apostles, all the followers and disciples of the Lord, all the ancient martyrs, all who in times past loved the Lord as their personal Savior and Redeemer, will help swell the population of the Eternal City. The writer of the Epistle to the Hebrews introduces all of them when he exclaims: "But ye are come unto Mount Sion and unto the city of the living God, the heavenly Jerusalem, and to an innumerable company of angels, to the general assembly and church of the first-born, which are written in heaven, and to God, the Judge of all, and to the spirits of just men made perfect and to Jesus, the Mediator of the New Covenant" (12:22-24). Oh, what delightful associations we shall enjoy in "yonder shining regions"! Some consider it quite an honor to be admitted into the society of the *élite* here on earth. But what is that compared with admission into the society of God's elect in the "city fair and high"!

> The patriarchs' and prophets' noble train
> With all Christ's followers true,
> Who bore the cross and could the worst disdain
> That tyrants dared to do,

9

I see them shine forever,
All glorious as the sun,
Mid light that fadeth never,
Their perfect freedom won.

All who have died in the Lord are in heaven. Death to the believer is the key that opens immediately the portals of heaven. As soon as the Christian dies, he goes to heaven. This the Apostle John tells us Rev. 14:13: "And I heard a voice from heaven saying unto me, Write, Blessed are the dead which die in the Lord *from henceforth.*" The moment the believer departs this life, he is transferred to the celestial mansions above. Indeed, his body is placed into the grave, where in the course of time it may molder away, turn to dust by decay; but his real self, that is, his spirit, wings away to realms beyond. Solomon assures us: "Then shall the dust return to the earth as it was, and *the spirit shall return unto God, who gave it*" (Eccl. 12:7). Hence the Lord promises the penitent malefactor on the cross, "Today shalt thou be with Me in paradise" (Luke 23:43). And the Apostle Paul triumphantly exclaims: "We are confident, I say, and willing rather to be absent from the body and to be present with the Lord" (2 Cor. 5:8). What a comfort to know that our dear departed who died in true faith are now in heaven, enjoying the company of Jesus and of the holy angels and of all God's beloved saints of ages past! They are at this moment standing before the throne of the great King, the Lord Jesus Christ. According to their soul they are already enjoying the privilege of eating "of the eternal manna" and of drinking "of the river of Thy [God's] pleasures forevermore", having now entered the heavenly Jerusalem together with all "the general assembly and church of the firstborn which are written in heaven".

Yes, the same bodies in which our souls dwelt here on earth. Job writes by inspiration of God: *"In my flesh* shall I see God, whom I shall see for myself and *mine eyes* shall behold, and not another" (19:26,27). On the day of resurrection the same bodies we had on earth will be made alive again. "But if the Spirit of Him that raised up Jesus from the dead dwell in you, He that raised up Christ from the dead shall also *quicken your mortal bodies* by His Spirit, that dwelleth in you," writes Paul (Rom. 8:11). And in the celebrated fifteenth chapter of his First Letter to the Corinthians he asserts: "For *this corruptible* must *put on incorruption,* and *this mortal* must *put on immortality"* (v. 53). This glorious hope the apostle bases on Christ's own resurrection from the dead; for in the twentieth verse of this same chapter he writes: "But now is Christ risen from the dead and become the *Firstfruits of them that slept."* Christ is the "Firstfruits," i. e., His resurrection from the dead is the beginning of a work to end only when the body of every child of God has been raised from its sleepingplace and brought home to glory. What a comforting fact this is! No matter where the dust of our body may have been deposited or scattered — in the sea or on the mountain or in the churchyard — it is safe. On the great Last Day it will be gathered again. With the same body which was subject to the weaknesses and afflictions of this life we shall share in the bliss and glory of the life to come in heaven. What a source of comfort regarding our loved ones whose bodies rest in the chambers of death! In Christ they now sleep; in Him they will also rise again. On the resurrection morning they will come forth from the graves where we laid them, the same dear ones that they were of old, with the same body, the same features, the same look of love in their eye and on their countenance, the same in all respects — yet marvelously transformed.

WHAT KIND OF BODIES SHALL WE HAVE IN HEAVEN?

The Scripture informs us that our bodies, though the same bodies that we had on earth, will experience a glorious change. Paul writes: "The dead shall be *raised incorruptible, and we shall be changed"* (1 Cor. 15:52). Just what this change will consist in the apostle tells us: "So also is the resurrection of the dead. It is sown in corruption, it is *raised in incorruption.* It is sown in dishonor, it is *raised in glory.* It is sown in weakness, it is *raised in power.* It is sown a natural body, it is *raised a spiritual body.* There is a natural body, and there is a spiritual body. . . . And as we have borne the image of the earthly, we shall also *bear the image of the heavenly.* Now, this I say, brethren, that flesh and blood cannot inherit the kingdom of God. Neither doth corruption inherit incorruption. . . . For this corruptible must *put on incorruption,* and this mortal must *put on immortality"* (1 Cor. 15:42-44, 49, 50, 53). Again, in describing this great change, the same apostle compares: "Who [Christ] shall change our vile body that it may be fashioned *like unto His glorious body,* according to the working whereby He is able even to subdue all things unto Himself" (Phil. 3:21). "Then shall the righteous," says Jesus, *"shine forth as the sun in the kingdom of their Father"* (Matt. 13:43). "They shall *hunger no more, neither thirst any more,* neither shall the sun light on them nor any heat." (Rev. 7:16)

According to these Scripture texts, then, our bodies are to experience a great change when we rise from our graves, just as a great change was wrought in the body of our Lord when He rose from the dead. Christ's body was the same after His resurrection and yet different; it was identical and yet changed; it was recognized by the disciples, and yet in some mysterious way it was no longer subject to the limitations, the restrictions, and the material wants of His former state of humiliation. He ate with His disciples, but not to satisfy bodily hunger. He merely wanted to prove to them that He had actually risen from the dead. He appeared to them even though the doors were locked and bolted. He appeared suddenly and just as suddenly disappeared. He instructed His followers to meet Him in Galilee, where He wished to give them the Great Commission; but He did not travel there with them. No, in some mysterious, supernatural, miraculous way He found His own way there, and before the disciples had arrived, He was waiting there to meet them. No wonder they were filled with awe when He appeared to them on Easter evening. We are not surprised that "they were terrified and affrighted and supposed that they had seen a spirit" (Luke 24:37). It was but a natural manifestation of their terror and reverence that they "held Him by the feet and worshiped Him." (Matt. 28:9)

Our resurrection bodies will be similar to the resurrection body of Christ. Paul assures us that Christ "shall change our vile body that it may be fashioned like unto His glorious body, according to the working whereby He is able even to subdue all things unto Himself" (Phil. 3:21). Just as His body was the same, though changed, so will our bodies be the same, though changed. As His body was no longer subject to the restrictions and limitations of His state of humiliation, so our bodies will be free from the chains of this mortal condition. As His body was delivered from the weariness, infirmities, and sufferings of preresurrection life, so our bodies will be delivered from the weaknesses, afflictions, and tribulations of earthly existence. As His body was no longer mortal, so our bodies will no longer be subject to death. No more tears, no more pain, no more sickness, no more death. "God shall wipe away all tears from their eyes, and there shall be no more death, neither sorrow nor crying, neither shall there be any more pain; for the former things are passed away" (Rev. 21:4). "Beloved, now are we the sons of God, and it doth not yet appear what we shall be; but we know that when He shall appear, we shall be like Him, for we shall see Him as He is." (1 John 3:2)

Oh, what a prospect is ours! We shall be like Jesus. Our dear departed dead will be like Jesus. Hopefully we sing with the Christian poet

My flesh shall slumber in the grave
Till the last trumpet's joyful sound;
Then burst the chains with sweet surprise
And in my Savior's image rise.

SHALL WE KNOW ONE ANOTHER IN HEAVEN?

This is a question which is often asked by those who through death have been compelled to give up a loved one. Will there actually be a reunion in heaven in which we shall recognize and know one another as we do on earth? Will a father recognize his children when they finally follow him to heaven? Shall we know our mother when we, too, enter the heavenly home? Shall we really know our sisters and brothers as well as those who were our friends and acquaintances in this life? Although the Bible does not answer this question one way or the other in so many words, we confidently believe that we shall know one another in heaven. Why may we believe this?

The Bible clearly teaches that the image of God given through Adam, the first man, but later lost through the fall into sin, will finally be fully restored in heaven. This we know from the psalmist: "I will behold Thy face in righteousness; I shall be satisfied, when I awake, *with Thy likeness*" (Ps. 17:15). In heaven the image, or likeness, of God will again be ours. The image of God includes not only perfect righteousness and holiness but also keen insight and remarkable knowledge of things. Having the image of God, Adam was able to recognize Eve at once, though he had never seen her before. According to Genesis 2 Eve was made from a rib of Adam while he slept. But no sooner had Eve been brought to Adam than he exclaimed: "This is now bone of my bones and flesh of my flesh; she shall be called woman because she was taken out of man" (Gen. 2:23). This image of God, which enabled Adam to recognize Eve and to assign names "to all cattle and to the fowl of the air and to every beast of the field," will also be ours when we reach heaven. With God's likeness restored to us in heaven, we may be sure that our senses of perception and knowledge of things and persons will be not inferior but equal to Adam's before the Fall. The image of God will enable us to recognize not only those whom we knew here on earth — parents, children, friends, and acquaintances — but also the patriarchs of old, the prophets and apostles, whom we never met personally on earth. The Bible relates that when the Lord Jesus manifested His divine glory to three disciples on the Mount of Transfiguration, His disciples immediately recognized Moses and Elijah, who appeared with the Lord in heavenly glory, even though they had never seen these two men of God before. May we not believe that, with our eye and mind and memory glorified, we shall be able to recognize our loved ones in heaven, yes, all saints of all ages? Were we not to know one another there, heaven's happiness would not measure up to the happiness we experience on earth through mutual contacts and associations. Here we are often obliged to ask, "Who is he?" In heaven such questions will no longer be necessary. Introductions will be a thing of the past.

A certain writer (Meyfart) has very beautifully described this aspect of heaven's bliss: "In heaven it will be said: There is the preacher who taught me, and there is the hearer who heeded me; there is the teacher who instructed me, and there is the pupil who so diligently studied; there is the governor who protected me, and there is the citizen who honored me; there is the master who kept me, and there is the servant who was subject unto me; there is the father who trained me, and there is the mother who nursed me; there is the pious child that obeyed us, and there is the brother who loved us; there is the friend and benefactor who gave me meat when I was an hungred, gave me drink when I was thirsty, clothed me when I was naked, comforted me when I was sad, took me in when I was banished, visited me when I was in prison, cared for me when I was sick." Here on earth, especially in larger cities, people living in the same block often remain strangers. In the heavenly city such a condition will not prevail. There we shall know and recognize all the saints, particularly our loved ones who departed this life truly believing in our Redeemer. There is no reason why we may not believe that parents will know their children and children their parents, that friendships formed here on earth will be renewed and continued in heaven.

Supposing, however, that this or that loved one is missing in heaven, will not the knowledge of that fact mar or at least diminish our joy of heaven? Not in the least. It caused Father Abraham no sadness whatsoever to know that the rich man, a fellow Jew and son after the flesh, was in hell, suffering torments. Nor will our happiness in heaven be disturbed by the absence of some relative or acquaintance. The will of all saints will conform to the will of God. And what is God's will? He wills that all who refuse to believe in Jesus Christ as their only Savior be denied admittance into heaven. "He that believeth not the Son shall not see life, but the wrath of God abideth on him" (John 3:36). There God's will is the will of all saints, all who have been "renewed in knowledge after the image of Him that created them" (Col. 3:10). Ties of earthly relationship will no longer influence our will in glory, but God's holiness and justice will guide all our thinking. God loved the lost with an everlasting love and therefore provided for them a way of salvation through Christ, His own dear Son, the Savior of all men; but since all those who are lost have spurned His love by rejecting their Savior through unbelief, God's justice must prevail. There is no alternative. As God wills, so also all saints in heaven will. Heaven is a place "wherein dwelleth righteousness." (2 Peter 3:13)

What great comfort we find in the thought of a reunion in heaven! There we shall find our loved ones again. Separation through death is but temporary. Some day, "some blessed day," all who have died in the Lord will reunite. What a happy occasion that will be! What a sweet comfort for us to know that these dear ones of ours will be in heaven, not indeed in the former relations of blood, but in the closer, happier relation of heaven, in blissful union with Christ, the Savior.

> The saints on earth and those above
> But one communion make;
> Joined to their Lord in bonds of love,
> All of His grace partake.
>
> One family, we dwell in Him,
> One Church above, beneath,
> Though now divided by the stream,
> The narrow stream of death.
>
> One army of the living God,
> To His commands we bow;
> Part of the host have passed the flood,
> And part are crossing now.
>
> Lo, thousands to their endless home
> Are swiftly borne away;
> And we are to the margin come
> And soon must launch as they.
>
> Lord Jesus, be our constant Guide;
> Then, when the word is given,
> Bid death's cold flood its waves divide
> And land us safe in heaven.

IS THERE EVIL IN HEAVEN?

As to this question the Bible gives us clear and definite information. There is no evil of any kind in heaven. Inhabitants of heaven are free from every evil of body and soul.

The greatest evil in this world is *sin,* the root of all evil.

18

Sin is the cause of all earthly misery and woe. If there were no sin, there would be no sickness, no pain, no heartaches, no disappointments, no death. Sin is the mother of every evil. *In heaven there is no sin.* When Paul was looking forward to departure from this life he wrote to Timothy: "Henceforth there is laid up for me a crown of *righteousness*" (2 Tim. 4:8). Peter spoke of heaven as "an inheritance incorruptible and *undefiled* and that fadeth not away" (1 Peter 1:4). In the Epistle to the Hebrews the saints in heaven are described as *"just men made perfect"* (Heb. 12:23). What a contrast between this world and our heavenly home! Here sin abounds; there holiness and righteousness prevail. Here everyone sins; there no one sins. Here we are surrounded by all manner of temptation to sin; there every temptation is forever excluded. Here even the Christian has to confess: "The good that I would I do not, but the evil which I would not, that I do" (Rom. 7:19); there even the slightest inclination to sin cannot disturb. Here sin causes us to lament: "O wretched man that I am!" (Rom. 7:24); there perfection permeates the whole being. What a glorious prospect! No sin, no imperfection, no taint of moral corruption! Heaven is a place of sinlessness. Its inhabitants are perfectly holy and without blemish.

Being free from sin, the saints are *free from every pain of this earthly existence.* Who can adequately describe the pains, heartaches, and sorrows to which mortal man is subject here on earth? This world is at best nothing but a vale of tears. As you walk along the streets of our cities, as you pass through our hospitals and similar institutions, as you read the columns of our daily newspapers, you cannot escape the fact that there is much misery and woe in the world. The poor clamor for food and raiment, the blind grope in darkness, the sick stretch out on beds of misery, the crippled are deprived of the use of the members of the body, worry drives many to untimely death. Now note how the Bible describes the absence of all these evils in heaven. The Apostle John offers consolation: "And God shall *wipe away all tears from their eyes;* and there shall be no more death, *neither sorrow* nor *crying,* neither shall there be *any more pain;* for the former things are passed away" (Rev. 21:4). "They shall *hunger no more, neither thirst* any more, neither shall the sun light on them *nor any heat*" (Rev. 7:16, 17). Hence complete deliverance from all pain of body and soul is the happy lot of all who enter heaven.

And, what is more, *there will be no more death.* Death is a merciless enemy. He spares no one. For centuries he has been stalking through the world, slaying unnumbered millions. He has desolated countless homes and broken billions of hearts. He is no respecter of persons. Children as well as adults are snatched away by him. The most intimate relationships are torn asunder by his ruthless power. How our hearts ache when we are forced to give up our loved ones! What bitter sorrow is caused by this relentless foe of the human race!

But in heaven "death is swallowed up in victory" (1 Cor. 15:54). "The last enemy that shall be destroyed is death" (1 Cor. 15:26). "And there shall be no more death" (Rev. 21:4). The saints in heaven are beyond the possibility of dying; for Jesus tells us (Luke 20:36): "Neither *can* they die any more, for they are equal unto the angels and are the children of God, being the children of the resurrection."

What a deliverance! No sin, no pain of any kind, no death, in heaven. When the Christian closes his eyes in death here on earth, he forever bids farewell to these enemies. "The

Egyptians pursued the Hebrews to the very shores of the sea. There, however, the people saw the last of those tyrants who had made life so bitter for them. In weltering waves from which they shrink back with dread, their enemies and their griefs are to find a common grave. God's people are like His ancient Israel. They have enemies who harass them in life and pursue them to the very shores of time. But the Christian's deathbed will be the death of them all. Death is their destruction, not ours. And how should it reconcile us to that dark and doleful passage from which nature shrinks that when we stand in its gloomy portal to take a last look at this fading world, we shall take our last look, not at friends in Christ — for we shall meet them again in heaven — but only at these our enemies! As Moses said of the doomed Egyptians, we 'shall see them again no more forever.'" Oh, how our hearts should leap for joy that in heaven we shall have done forever with all the evils of this life!

What Are the Outstanding Joys of Heaven?

That heaven is a place of unspeakable joy is attested in innumerable passages of Holy Writ. The prospect of joy in heaven is not a figment of Christian imagination. It is happy reality. God's Word vouches for it. In Ps. 16:11 we read: "In Thy presence is *fullness of joy;* at Thy right hand there are pleasures forevermore." The prophet Isaiah writes: "The ransomed of the Lord shall return and come to Zion with songs and *everlasting joy upon their heads;* they shall obtain *joy and gladness,* and sorrow and sighing shall flee away" (35:10). The Lord Jesus once said to His disciples: "Blessed are ye that weep now, *for ye shall laugh"* (Luke 6:21). The psalmist refers to the same heavenly joy which the Christian experiences after the sorrows of this life when he exclaims in Ps. 126:5,6: "They that sow in tears *shall reap in joy.* He that goeth forth and weepeth, bearing precious seed, shall doubtless come again with *rejoicing,* bringing his sheaves with him." The tears of God's children here are followed by laughter there. Our mouth will be filled with laughter and our tongue with singing. Even here we rejoice when we think of God's unmerited kindness and the unspeakable grace which He has bestowed upon us through Christ, our Savior. But this our joy is too often mingled with sadness, marred by sin. In heaven, however, there will be "fullness of joy," joy complete, without alloy. "Ye shall laugh," says Jesus. Yes, there will be laughter in heaven, pure, holy, heavenly laughter. There will be no sour faces, no downcast spirits, no gloom or sadness. A perpetual smile of joy will light up the countenances of the redeemed. Heaven's happiness will be "undefiled." (1 Peter 1:4)

Why do the saints rejoice so in heaven? What is the cause of their happiness? What are their outstanding joys? First of all, *they see God.* What joy unspeakable to see face to face Him who loved them with an everlasting love, who provided for them a way of salvation through His own dear Son, and who graciously kept them in the faith unto the end, so that they have received the crown of life! Who can begin to describe the joy that fills the hearts of the ransomed when, basking in the sunshine of God's presence, they are permitted to thank and praise Him forevermore for His marvelous grace toward the children of men? John writes: "Beloved, now are we the sons of God, and it doth not yet appear what we shall be; but we know that, when He shall appear, we shall be like Him; for *we shall see Him as He is"* (1 John 3:2). Job exultantly rejoices when speaking of his resurrection: "In my flesh shall I *see God*" (Job 19:26). The Apostle John describes the chief joy of the saints in heaven when he says of them: "And *God Himself shall be with them* and be their God" (Rev. 21:3). God is the Source of endless joy; in Him there is nothing to call forth sadness or any unhappiness; therefore, to be in His presence affords the inhabitants of heaven unending bliss.

We shall see Jesus. Our precious Savior will be in heaven, and we shall be with Him there. Paul assures the Thessalonian Christians: "And so shall we ever *be with the Lord*" (1 Thess. 4:17). Jesus Himself prays: "Father, I will that they also whom Thou hast given Me *be with Me* where I am" (John 17:24). No wonder the Apostle Paul longs for the heavenly home; for there he is to *"be with Christ,* which is far better"* (Phil. 1:23). What a thrilling experience it will be to meet Jesus face to face! Here in this life it is Jesus who is the All in all of every true Christian's heart. Jesus so loved us that He did not shrink from the greatest sacrifices to make it possible for us to reach heaven. He left His heavenly throne of glory and assumed human form to be our Savior and Redeemer. Jesus endured poverty, ridicule, suffering, and even the shameful death of a malefactor, that He might atone for our sins. "Greater love hath no man than this, that a man lay down his life for his friends," says Jesus (John 15:13). But He did more; He laid down His life for us who through sin had become His enemies. Greater love than that which Jesus manifested toward fallen, sinful mankind can nowhere be found. What joy unspeakable it will be in heaven to see Jesus, to talk to Jesus, and to thank Jesus personally for His undying love! Then the walls of the celestial mansions will reverberate

23

with the anthems of thanksgiving of all the saints. The Apostle John in his vision of heaven tells us that there will be harps and golden vials full of odors and a new song. The saints will sing: "Thou art worthy, O Lord, to receive glory and honor and power; . . . for Thou wast slain and hast redeemed us to God by Thy blood out of every kindred, and tongue, and people, and nation and hast made us unto our God kings and priests" (Rev. 4:11; 5:9, 10). Music and song and worship of Jesus shall there swell every heart. A chorus of endless praise to the glory of our Redeemer will resound through the heavenly corridors forever and ever. What a happy experience it will be to have a part in this celestial chorus! O blessed home of the redeemed! "How the thought of what it is enkindles the desire to break loose at once from all the entanglements of earth, to lay aside the body, to soar aloft, and to enter speedily its waiting gates of pearl!" To see Jesus face to face, to revel in His divine tenderness forever, and to adore Him throughout the endless ages of eternity for His divine love toward us, this will be the chief joy of the inhabitants of heaven, the very pinnacle of heavenly bliss and happiness. No wonder the poet longs to be away from the earth with all its labors and sorrows and to "be at rest," where sin is unknown and where sorrow never comes. He sings

> Jerusalem, my happy home!
> My soul still pants for thee;
> Then shall my labors have an end
> When I thy joys shall see.

How Do We Get To Heaven?

This is indeed a vital question. The Scriptural information given in answer to all the foregoing questions will be of no real benefit to you if you are not able to answer this one. There are very few people who do not wish to go to heaven when they die. Most people delight in hearing of that bright and shining city on yonder shore. They speak of their loved ones as being there and hope someday to meet them again. But wishing and desiring to go to heaven is not enough. We must definitely know how we can get to heaven. The Bible tells us in such simple language that all can understand.

Between heaven and man is a barrier which must be removed. That barrier is *sin*. Man has sinned and thus forfeited his right to enter heaven. This applies to all men without exception. "There is no difference," says Scripture, "for all have sinned and come short of the glory of God" (Rom. 3: 22, 23). Even outwardly moral and respectable men are not without sin. "If we say we have no sin, we deceive ourselves, and the truth is not in us" (1 John 1:8). Sin makes man unfit for heaven. Sin merits God's punishment, death: "The wages of sin is death" (Rom. 6:23). "The soul that sinneth, it shall die" (Ezek. 18:20). Because of sin man deserves hell, not heaven.

Thank God there is One who has bridged the gulf that separates sinful man from heaven. Jesus Christ atoned for the sins of all men. He paid the penalty of sin by suffering and dying as all men's Substitute. He won forgiveness of sin by suffering the punishment of sin. *Jesus, therefore, is the one and only Way to heaven.* He tells us in His holy Word: "I am the Way, the Truth, and the Life; no man cometh unto the Father but by Me" (John 14:6). As Noah's ark was the only place of safety at the time of that terrible catastrophe, the Deluge, and as Joseph was the only man who could supply food at the time of the Egyptian famine, so Jesus Christ is the

25

only Way to heaven. "Neither is there salvation in any other; for there is none other name under heaven given among men whereby we must be saved" (Acts 4:12). Would you go to heaven? Then believe in Christ as your personal Savior, who has suffered the punishment also of your sins. Accept by faith the forgiveness of sin which He has won also for you and which He offers you in the Gospel. Follow the apostle's instructions once given to the Philippian jailer: "Believe on the Lord Jesus Christ, and thou shalt be saved" (Acts 16:31). Remember, "he that believeth on the Son hath everlasting life; and he that believeth not the Son shall not see life, but the wrath of God abideth on him" (John 3:36). "God so loved the world that He gave His only-begotten Son, that whosoever believeth in Him should not perish, but have everlasting life." (John 3:16)

Your virtues and your morality will not get you to heaven, because you have sinned and sin causes God to punish the sinner. Your good character before men will not get you to heaven; for you have sinned and sin deserves God's wrath and condemnation. The only way you can get to heaven is by trusting in Christ as your Savior from sin. Oh, how many foolishly trust in their works, believing that through them they may gain heaven! Spurgeon tells of an old coachman who once had him for a passenger in his cab. As the famous pastor entered the vehicle, he dropped a remark concerning the cabman's age and then added: "Well, I hope you have seen to it that yours will be a pleasant lot when this life comes to an end." "Yes, sir," the old coachman replied, "I think I have; for, as far as I know, I have never been drunk in my life, I have never used a profane word, and I also go to church occasionally." He seemed quite satisfied with himself and was much surprised when Spurgeon told him that he would never reach heaven if he should die in such a self-righteous state of mind.

How many there are who build their hope of getting to heaven on what they have done! But heaven can never be reached in that way. We are saved solely by God's grace through faith in Jesus Christ. The Christian hymn expresses this great truth most beautifully in the words

> Not the labors of my hands
> Can fulfill Thy Law's demands.
> Could my zeal no respite know,
> Could my tears forever flow,
> All for sin could not atone;
> Thou must save, and Thou alone.

Heaven is a gift, the gift of God through Jesus Christ. It cannot be bought. It can never be merited by sinful man. "The *gift* of God is eternal life through Jesus Christ, our Lord" (Rom. 6:23). From the *Lutheran Annual* of some years ago we cite the following to illustrate the truth of the passage just quoted from Scripture:

During the Spanish War, Colonel Roosevelt commanded a regiment of Rough Riders in Cuba. He became much attached to his men and was greatly concerned when a number of them fell sick.

Hearing that Miss Clara Barton (the lady who devoted herself to the work of nursing the wounded soldiers) had received a supply of delicacies for the invalids under her care, Colonel Roosevelt requested her to sell a portion of them to him for the sick men of his regiment.

His request was refused. The Colonel was very much

27

troubled; he cared for his men and was willing to pay for the supplies out of his own pocket.

"How can I get these things?" he asked. "I must have proper food for my sick men."

"Just ask for them, Colonel."

"Oh," said Roosevelt, his face breaking into a smile, "that's the way, is it? Then I do ask for them." And he got them at once.

How often Roosevelt's mistake is repeated by many in the matter of salvation! People seem to expect to receive heaven in exchange for something that they can offer. One brings an earnest prayer; a second brings a vow or pledge to turn over a new leaf; a third brings a resolution to live a better and a purer life; a fourth thinks that before he can be saved, he must produce some evidence of his sincerity by improvement in his conduct; a fifth imagines that he can obtain this great blessing by conforming to certain religious observances.

Now, the truth is that God's salvation can be had only as a free gift. Pride rebels against this. It would rather pay, however small the price. But God is too great to sell His blessing, nor could any man merit it in the smallest degree, however long he might try. But God is prepared to meet the sinner with His hands *full* of richest blessings if only the sinner will come with *empty* hands to receive them.

Yes, "the gift of God is eternal life through Jesus Christ, our Lord." (Rom. 6:23)

What Is Meant By
Degrees and Differences in Heaven?

By this are meant the degrees in glory and the differences in the rewards of grace. That there will be a difference in the rewards of grace the Apostle Paul indicates when he writes: "He which soweth sparingly shall reap also sparingly; and he which soweth bountifully shall reap also bountifully" (2 Cor. 9:6). Paul is speaking of believing Christians, who manifest their faith by works of love; for instance, by giving for the Lord's cause. Some Christians sow sparingly, giving but meagerly, while others sow abundantly, giving generously, in proportion as God has prospered them. All Christians will reap, but the latter, by grace, will reap more abundantly than the former. They will shine more brightly than those who were chary of works of love and only with difficulty could be persuaded to participate in charitable endeavors. The apostle refers to this difference in glory in another passage of Scripture, 1 Cor. 15:41, 42, where he writes: "There is one glory of the sun and another glory of the moon and another glory of the stars; for one star differeth from another star in glory. So also is the resurrection of the dead." The apostle evidently means to say: Just as the heavenly bodies, the sun, the moon, the stars, differ among themselves in beauty and brightness, so in heaven there will be differences in the brightness of the glory to be bestowed upon all saints. All will be glorious, but there will be degrees of glory. Some will shine brighter than others. The reward of grace given those who have sown bountifully will be greater than that received by such as have sown sparingly. Besides admitting all believers in Christ into heaven by grace, God, in His immeasurable kindness and mercy, grants additional glory to those of His saints who have given more abundant evidence of their faith by their labors of love for Him and their fellow men. All glory is by grace; none is merited. The Apostle Paul as well as the thief on the cross is saved solely by God's grace. Heaven is a gift to the former as well as to the latter. By grace and by grace alone both will be glorious in heaven; but the glory of Paul will be greater than that of the penitent thief. For such as have been instrumental in leading others to heaven the reward of grace will be particularly great. "And they that be wise [that teach others the way to eternal life] shall shine as the brightness of the firmament and they that turn many to righteousness as the stars forever and ever." (Dan. 12:3)

This unmerited kindness of God should be an incentive to every Christian to give, to work, to suffer, to the limit of his God-given ability. "Great is your reward in heaven" (Matt. 5:12). Though we in no wise deserve it, the Lord will greatly reward even the gift of a cup of cold water given to a thirsty and needy fellow mortal. Therefore, as an old inscription puts it

> For our Lord Jesus Christ's sake
> Do all the good you can
> To all the people you can,
> By all the means you can,
> In all the places you can,
> As long as ever you can.

Heaven — what a delightful subject to contemplate! We need not sorrow, "even as others which have no hope" (1 Thess. 4:13). By faith in our Savior heaven is assured to us as it is already the eternal possession of our dear ones who have entered its pearly gates and are now enjoying its indescribable glory. We, too, shall some day share its bliss with those who have gone before. "So shall we ever be with the Lord" (1 Thess. 4:17) and with those whom we love.

> I'm but a stranger here,
> Heaven is my home;

Earth is a desert drear,
Heaven is my home;
Danger and sorrow stand
Round me on every hand;
Heaven is my fatherland,
Heaven is my home.

What though the tempest rage,
Heaven is my home;
Short is my pilgrimage,
Heaven is my home;
And time's wild wintry blast
Soon shall be overpast;
I shall reach home at last,
Heaven is my home.

There at my Savior's side
Heaven is my home;
I shall be glorified,
Heaven is my home.
There are the good and blest,
Those I love most and best;
And there I, too, shall rest,
Heaven is my home.

Therefore I murmur not,
Heaven is my home;
Whate'er my earthly lot,
Heaven is my home;
And I shall surely stand
There at my Lord's right hand.
Heaven is my fatherland,
Heaven is my home.

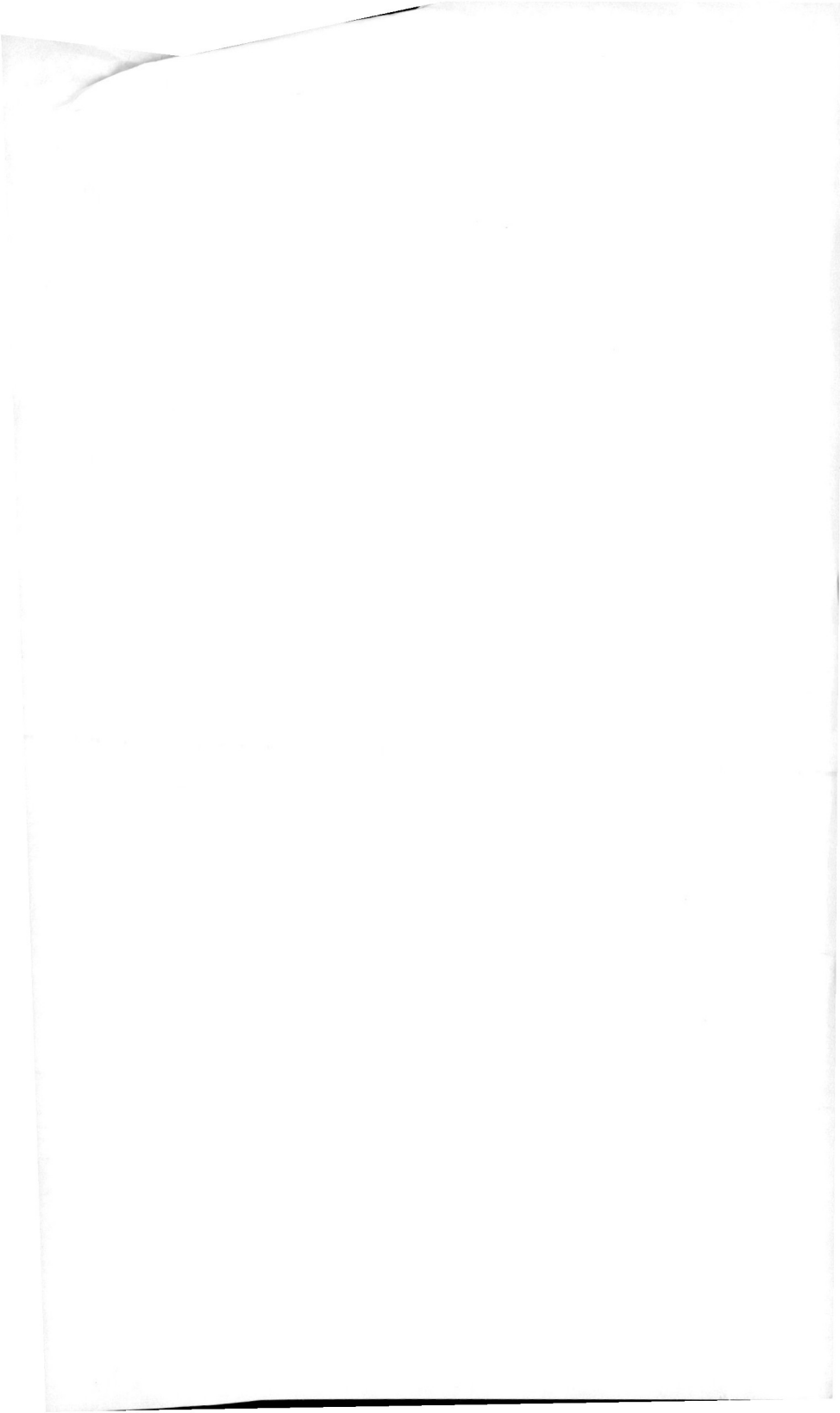

www.ingramcontent.com/pod-product-compliance
Lightning Source LLC
Chambersburg PA
CBHW031226090426
42740CB00007B/734